Rethinking
Golf Clubs
with
Phil Moore

An inside perspective on
the confusing
and very misunderstood
world of golf clubs

Special Thanks!

To three friends who helped
me create this little book

Jerry Honstein
My eagle-eyed editor

Jeanne Hartman
My hard-working photographer

Mike Wood
For helping me put all the
pieces together

Hello, let me introduce myself

My name is Philip Moore. I own and operate *Phil's Custom Golf Shop*, located in "The Nest" at the beautiful Goose Creek Golf Club in Mira Loma, California.

In addition to being a professional golf club fitter and builder, I'm also a golf coach and golf writer. I'm a member of both the *Association of Golf Clubfitting Professionals* (AGCP) and the *International Clubmakers Guild* (IGC). In addition to writing this book, I've written two others, *The Mad Science of Golf: On moving past golf industry hype and learning to play better golf*, published in 2007, and *Understanding Golf: Learn to significantly lower your average score without hitting the ball farther, changing your swing, or buying expensive golf clubs*, published in 2012.

You'll find me most often working in my shop or teaching somewhere on the Goose Creek Golf Course or practice facility. I most enjoy helping average soulful golfers grow their game.

I look forward to meeting you.

Phil Moore
PhilsGolf.com
951-377-6268

Why I wrote this book

I've been fitting, building, and repairing golf clubs for well over 20 years. I wrote this book to provide the reader with a glimpse into what I've discovered to be true.

It's a simple little book with no filler. On each page, I offer one idea that I would like you to consider. The book can easily be read in a single setting but, if you're in a hurry, you can actually read it in a matter of minutes.

*Just read the question, the answer,
and the bold italicized sentences
on each page.*

It ain't what you don't know that gets you in trouble. It's what you know for sure that just ain't so.

Mark Twain

Contents

Thoughts About Golf Clubs

2   **Are golf clubs really getting better every year?**
No, they just look different.

4   **So what happens if I don't keep up with the new technology?**
You save money.

5   **Is there a best brand of golf club?**
No, some brands just cost more.

6   **Why are new brand-name golf clubs so expensive?**
Marketing is expensive and you're the one paying for it.

7   **Are designer-name putters worth the added cost?**
Possibly, if you're a collector.

8   **If golf clubs are as good as they're going to get, why do manufacturers keep coming up with new designs every year?**
They've created a market for the myth of "new technology".

9   **If the newest designs are no better, why do touring professionals always play them?**
They don't always play them, and those that do are generally under contract.

10   **So why do touring professionals continue to improve?**
The question should be, why hasn't the average golfer EVER improved?

12   **Why don't average golfers just buy
older designs?**
*They should and, after reading this book,
hopefully they will.*

13   **So the new brand-name golf clubs
are overrated?**
*With regards to how much they'll improve
your game, very overrated.*

14   **Are forged iron heads the best?**
No, they're just more expensive.

15   **Do golfers "over think" golf clubs?**
To the point that it inhibits their ability to improve.

Thoughts About Golf Club Fitting

18   **So is golf club fitting overrated as well?**
No, the fit is everything.

19   **Does everyone fit golf clubs the same way?**
No, almost everyone fits golf clubs differently.

21   **Should the golf club fitter have a good
understanding of swing mechanics?**
*Yes, otherwise the fitting process will be
nothing more than "fit by numbers".*

23   **Is the shaft the engine of the golf club?**
No, it's the most overrated part of the golf club.

25   **When selecting a shaft, is flex
the most important consideration?**
*No. Shaft length and shaft weight are more
important considerations.*

27   **How important is grip size and condition?**
More important than most golfers realize.

28   **Can I get fitted for golf clubs that will perfectly fit my swing?**
No. You're not a mechanical swing machine.

29   **Then why should I get fitted for golf clubs?**
Because a poorly fitted set makes golf more difficult than it already is.

30   **So, a properly fitted set of golf clubs will NOT make me a better golfer?**
Correct. You'll unfortunately still be the same golfer.

31   **What is the most common club fitting mistake?**
Not getting properly fitted for the most important clubs in the bag.

33   **Can I just make a few positive adjustments to the clubs I already have?**
Certainly and, if needed, you should.

Thoughts About YOUR Golf Clubs

36   **Do I really need to be fitted for my putter?**
Only if you would like to putt better.

38   **What driver should I be playing?**
A driver that provides MAXIMUM accuracy and adequate distance.

40   **Should I be fitted for my wedges?**
Yes, and the specifications should complement your properly fitted iron set.

42   **What iron design do you most often recommend?**
          A game improvement design with adequate loft.

44   **What would be the best set composition for me?**
          One that provides functional yardage gaps and playable trajectories throughout the bag.

Final Thoughts

48   **Four things you need to remember about golf clubs.**

50   **I look forward to helping you grow your game!**

Thoughts About Golf Clubs

*Some players are never satisfied unless
they are buying new clubs ...
This is not good for the player,
but it is quite good for the clubmaker.*

**James Braid
Five-time British Open Champion
between 1901 and 1910**

Are golf clubs really getting better every year?

No, they just look different.

Most golfers define a better golf club as one which will help them achieve lower scores. With that definition, you'd have to conclude that golf clubs are not getting better at all. If, each year, the newest design in golf clubs was able to save you just one stroke per round, you could improve through doing nothing more than continuously buying new golf clubs. Every year your handicap would automatically drop by a stroke.

That obviously has not happened and never will happen. Even though golf clubs are redesigned each year, they will never again offer the average golfer a meaningful benefit in performance. This is because to produce a legal golf club, manufacturers have to stay within the very strict guidelines set forth by the United States Golf Association (USGA) and The Royal & Ancient Golf Club of St. Andrews, Scotland (R&A). These two governing bodies of golf are highly committed to protecting the integrity of the game. They have no interest in softening their rules. They're not going to allow golf club designers to make the game easier than it was intended to be.

The ruling bodies of golf have thankfully tied the manufacturers' hands.

For example, while new driver heads may look different and offer increased adjustability, they cannot be designed to be any more forgiving than they already are. Furthermore, the driver face cannot be designed to launch the ball any faster than it already does.

Now, there will always be changes in golf club design, but those changes are market driven and primarily cosmetic. Just because golf clubs look different every year, and are given a different name, doesn't mean they're getting better.

So what happens if I don't keep up with the new technology?

You save money.

Today, the phrase "New Technology" has evolved into a marketing tool employed throughout the golf industry. It's used because (amazingly) it continues to work. Manufacturers have golfers convinced that they need to continuously purchase new golf clubs just to keep up with the "new technology". But, what value does this never-ending "new technology" really offer?

While today's golf equipment (especially the ball) is vastly superior to the equipment used 50 years ago, the average handicap is essentially the same.

Why hasn't the average golfer improved? The answer is clear.

Golf is not about technology.

Golf is a game. It's played. Improvement requires that you improve your playing skills, not your golf clubs. Unfortunately, the newest "high tech" golf club still does not select the shot, aim itself, or swing itself. Those skills are left to the golfer, who's no better than he was 50 years ago.

Is there a best brand of golf club?

No, some brands just cost more.

If there was a best brand of golf club, every professional golfer, on every tour in the world, would be playing it. Professionals realize that there is not one brand that is superior to all the others. It's the specifications of their golf clubs that professionals are concerned with. They want their clubs built to the specifications that help them achieve their desired feel, ball flight, and carry distances.

It's your golf club's specifications that you should be concerned with as well. Not the name stamped on the head.

Recently, an extremely expensive brand of golf clubs entered the market. Golfers are led to believe that the clubs they had been playing over the years were the equivalent to Toyota Camrys. Now, for a lot more money, they have the opportunity to upgrade to a Lexus.

From a playing standpoint (which is the only thing that matters) these very expensive golf clubs are no better at all. That's because to be deemed legal,

even the most expensive brand of golf clubs has to stay within the strict design guidelines established by the USGA and R&A.

Why are brand-name golf clubs so expensive?

Marketing is expensive and you're the one paying for it.

While the cost to manufacture golf clubs is relatively inexpensive (because it's done almost entirely out of the country), the marketing costs are enormous. An effective global advertising campaign is not cheap. Neither is paying the top players throughout the world a small fortune to play your equipment.

These marketing costs are passed along to the consumer, which is why purchasing new brand-name golf clubs will always be expensive. You're led to believe, however, that the added cost is justified because you're also paying for the research, development and precision manufacturing that's necessary to produce such a cutting-edge piece of equipment.

That sounds great, but the truth is that you're paying for marketing.

As long as golf club manufacturers continue to budget huge amounts of money for marketing, new brand-name golf clubs will continue to be expensive.

But marketing costs are their problem, not yours. If you're not interested in paying a lot of money for advertising, don't buy new brand-name clubs. It's that simple.

Are designer-name putters worth the added cost?

Possibly, if you're a collector.

Some golf clubs, primarily putters, bear the designer's name. It's a marketing tool that manufacturers love, because a designer's name can't be copied by the competition.

Designer name putters are positioned to represent unparalleled quality. A position that is supported by the fact that golfers see these putters being played regularly on the PGA and LPGA Tours. The actual benefits these putters provide to the tour players, however, is the fitting session in the designer's studio. Each putter is custom built to ideally fit the professional's eye, setup position, stroke, and sense of feel.

Unfortunately, when you buy an expensive designer name putter, the fitting session and custom build is not included in the purchase price. All you get is an over-priced putter, built to standard specifications, with the designer's name stamped on it. And, of course, a cool-looking head cover.

As with any golf club,

you need to forget about brand-name and focus on specifications.

If golf clubs are as good as they're going to get, why do manufacturers keep coming up with new designs every year?

They've created a market for the myth of "new technology".

Golfers have been led to believe that last year's designs are "old technology" and are therefore, in some way, not as good.

The same golfers believe that the newest designs represent "new technology" and are therefore, in some way, better.

The bottom line is...

... most golfers believe in the myth of "new technology" and many are willing to pay for it.

Realizing this, manufacturers continuously push their marketing departments to every year come up with new names, colors, and designs. They then position the finished product as "new/superior technology" and price it as though it is.

If the newest designs are no better, why do touring professionals always play them?

They don't always play them, and those that do are generally under contract.

It would be quite difficult to sell new, expensive "high tech" golf clubs if the best players in the world were playing older designs. The "high tech" myth would soon fade away, the truth would become apparent, and the golf club industry would take a major hit.

To prevent this from happening, most touring professionals are offered lucrative endorsement contracts, requiring them to play the newest designs.

Professionals are more than happy to accept the money because the clubs are always built to their exact specifications.

The vast majority of players on every tour are bound by the terms and conditions of an equipment endorsement contract. It's a win for the manufacturers, a win for the players, and "smoke and mirrors" for the consumer.

So why do touring professionals continue to improve?

The question should be, why hasn't the average golfer EVER improved?

The best players in the world are better than ever. The primary reason, according to golf club manufacturers, is once again related to "new technology".

Well, the average golfer has been buying all this "new technology" for the past 30 years, and what has happened to him? Why hasn't he improved?

It's true that the best players in the world are better than ever. Not only in golf, but in every sport. They're bigger, faster, stronger, and better trained. And, more importantly, they're continuingly learning how to "play" their respective games better.

When I was growing up, the typical PGA Touring professional was a slightly over-weight American, who smoked and seemed to spend as much time in the cocktail lounge as the driving range. Today, PGA Touring professionals are athletes, coming from every corner of the world. When not playing or practicing, they can often be found working with a sports psychologist to strengthen their mind, or working with their personal trainer to strengthen their body. They're all business.

Due to the higher level of competition, today's touring professionals have done WHAT THE AVERAGE GOLFER HAS NEVER DONE – they've improved their playing skills. They've become better golfers.

While better equipment has certainly helped, the truth is that it's only been the icing on the cake. The higher level of competition has *forced* players to learn how to lower their average score. If they wanted to stay employed, they had no choice.

Better equipment does not *force* players to improve their playing skills, competition does.

So why don't average golfers just buy older designs?

They should and, after reading this book, hopefully they will.

For manufacturers, identifying older designs as "old technology" is a double-edged sword. While it helps them sell new designs, the value of their older models drops like a rock. After all, who wants to buy "old technology"?

This is great news for the consumer, because ...

... the older designs are typically every bit as good (and sometimes even better) than the new designs. And they're available for a fraction of their original retail price.

The downside to purchasing older clubs is that you'll have to pay to have them adjusted to your personal specifications. The total savings will still be quite substantial.

So new brand-name golf clubs are overrated?

With regards to how much they'll improve your game, very overrated.

To be deemed legal, we know that golf club design has to stay within the guidelines established by the ruling bodies of golf, the USGA and R&A. For that reason, from a game-improvement standpoint, golf clubs have not improved for quite some time.

When you purchase new brand-name golf clubs, you're led to believe you're paying for the newest "game improvement technology".

But that is not true.

When you purchase new brand-name golf clubs, you're paying primarily for the newest "marketing hype".

Are forged iron heads better?

No, they're just more expensive.

The word "forged" has turned into a marketing tool similar to the phrase "new technology". Golfers have been led to believe that "forged" means "better" and, therefore, worth the additional price.

While it's true that manufacturing forged club heads is more costly than manufacturing cast club heads, cast club heads are certainly not inferior.

If fact, the casting process provides designers with the ability to create very deep cavity backs with extreme perimeter weighting. These "extreme" game improvement specifications cannot be achieved through forging.

Forged iron heads do, however, provide features that some players prefer over maximum forgiveness. For example, some players believe that the typical compact forged head provides better feel, looks better at address, and provides them with the ability to more easily shape shots (hit fades and draws).

While these features are important to some golfers, they are of little value to most. In fact ...

... when purchasing forged irons, most golfers are simply paying more money for a less forgiving club head.

To me, that doesn't make much sense.

Do golfers "over think" golf clubs?

To the point that it inhibits their ability to improve.

Golfers have been led to believe that golf clubs can do far more than is possible. Golf clubs do not swing themselves.

A new $500 brand-name driver will not swing itself faster and drive the ball 20 yards farther than last year's model. A $400 designer-name putter will not read the green, align itself to the intended line, and stroke the putt into the hole. And the weird looking sand wedge advertised on TV will not pop the ball out of the sand trap and safely onto the green every time.

You cannot buy the ability to create golf shots, it's a learned skill. And creating successful golf shots on the course is an art that requires not only skill, but also imagination and an understanding of how the game is best played.

When golfers become overly focused on their equipment, they stop improving.

Golfers striving to lower their average score need to focus more on their ball-striking and playing skills. And less on their equipment.

Thoughts About Golf Club Fitting

Everything that can be counted does not necessarily count; everything that counts cannot necessarily be counted.

Albert Einstein

So is golf club fitting overrated as well?

No, the fit is everything.

Once you understand that the design of a golf club is never going to meaningfully improve, you'll understand that ...

... the fit is all there is.

Does everyone fit golf clubs the same way?

No, almost everyone fits golf clubs differently.

Golf club fitters are similar to swing instructors in the sense that each one has their own idea on how to best perform their job. Just as you can go to three different swing instructors and get three different opinions on how to improve your golf swing, you can go to three different fitters and get three different opinions about the golf clubs you should be playing.

Because the fit is everything, you need to choose your fitter carefully.

Your first step would be to find a fitter whose primary interest is helping you lower your average score, as opposed to simply making a sale. Those fitters are hard to find in high-volume retail operations where success is measured in terms of sales.

A professional fitter can clearly articulate his objectives. When fitting a golfer, I have three goals. I refer to them as my "Three C's".

Comfort.
The grip's size and taper should feel *comfortable* in the player's hands. Each shaft length should allow the player to *comfortably* assume an effective address position. And, when swinging, the player should feel comfortable with the club's balance, as well as the weight and flex of the shaft.

Composition.
The set composition (the combination of wedges, irons, hybrids, and fairway metals) should provide the player with playable trajectories, functional yardage gaps, and a progressive series of predictable carry distances.

Compensation.
The specifications of each club should compensate for the player's most common miss. The goal is to reduce the severity of that miss: to help the player turn a percentage of his below average shots into average shots.

Should the golf club fitter have a good understanding of swing mechanics?

Yes, otherwise the fitting process is nothing more than "fit by numbers".

There is no mystery as to why the ball flies the way it does; it's a matter of *cause and effect.* The impact dynamics (cause) creates the ball flight (effect).

The ball is typically in contact with the club face for *about* three-quarters of an inch and *around* 5/10,000th of a second. The impact conditions during that brief instant will determine the ball flight. The goal of the fitting process is to provide the client with clubs that will improve those conditions.

Golf clubs, however, do not swing themselves. And, unfortunately, a golfer is not a mechanical swing machine. Realizing this, a professional fitter will always start the fitting process by analyzing the client's swing motion and impact "tendencies".

Then, before focusing on golf club specifications, the fitter will work with the client to improve the quality and consistency of those "tendencies". If needed, he'll make very subtle changes to the client's setup position (alignment, grip, ball position, and/or posture) and club delivery (the path on which the client most commonly delivers the club head to the ball).

A less qualified fitter will be unaware of how to effectively work with either the client's setup position or swing motion. As a result, the value of the fitting session will be limited because the fitter's

21

recommendations will be based solely on the numbers generated by the launch monitor.

This approach is commonly practiced at high-volume retail stores. It's a less effective fitting process that I refer to as being "fit by numbers".

Often questionable numbers.

Is the shaft the "engine" of the golf club?

No, the shaft is the most overrated part of the golf club.

A golf club has only three components, a grip, a shaft, and a head. Most golfers consider the shaft to be the "engine" of the golf club, and thus the most important component.

Contrary to popular belief, the shaft is neither an engine, nor the most important part of the golf club. The head – *by far* – is the most important component.

The shaft doesn't snap the ball forward (like a slingshot), or square the club face to the target at impact (as if it knew where the target was). And, needless to say, a very expensive shaft does not do both.

Also, a stiffer shaft doesn't stabilize the club head at impact, as so many golfers believe. Remember, the club head is in contact with the ball for only about 5/10,000th of a second. On off-center strikes, the club head will twist as though it was not even connected to a shaft. By the time the shaft stabilizes the head, the ball will have already launched off the club face.

Having said all this, the shaft's length, weight, flex, and bend profile will certainly affect the feel and playability of the golf club. Therefore, selecting the appropriate shaft specifications is an important step in the club fitting process.

Don't be misled, however, into believing a shaft can do more than it is capable of doing.

The shaft's overall importance is greatly overrated. It's not an engine and it's certainly not as important as the club head.

When selecting a golf shaft, is flex the most important consideration?

No. Shaft weight and shaft length are more important considerations.

Contrary to what most golfers believe, shaft length and shaft weight will generally influence impact conditions more than shaft flex.

Furthermore, it's easy to fit for shaft weight and shaft length because both are easily measured. Shaft flex, on the other hand isn't easy to measure at all. In fact, defining the flex of a particular shaft is left completely to the discretion of the individual manufacturer. There are no industry standards. As a result, one manufacturer's regular flex might play identical to a second manufacturer's senior flex, or a third manufacturer's stiff flex.

Adding to the confusion, each manufacturer measures shaft torque and shaft bend profile (the relative measurements of the shaft's tip section, mid section, and butt section) differently as well.

When I first started playing golf, over 50 years ago, the golfer never knew what he was getting until he went out and gave the club a try. When it comes to shaft flex, the same is true today. You have to forget about the labels on the shaft and test a variety of shafts with an open mind.

For most golfers, shaft flex influences feel more than anything else.

So my advice is this ...

... get fitted for the appropriate shaft weight and length. Then try different flexes and bend profiles until you find the shaft that FEELS best to you.

Then, keep that shaft and make all future adjustments to the head.

How important is grip size and condition?

More important than most realize.

The grip size, taper, and condition will influence both how tightly the golfer has to grip the club and how he aligns his hands on the grip. Both of these factors will influence how quickly the clubface rotates through the impact zone and, therefore, the golfer's ability to square the club face at impact.

Poorly sized or worn grips can lead to a loss of both power and control. As a general rule, golf clubs should be re-gripped about once a year or after every 40 rounds.

When it's time to re-grip your clubs,
if you've never done so, take the time to be properly fitted.

Can I get fitted for golf clubs that will perfectly fit my swing?

No. You're not a mechanical swing machine.

While golfers continually search for the golf clubs that perfectly fit their swing, they're forgetting that they're not a mechanical swing machine. They're a human swing machine that never swings the golf club exactly the same way twice.

So while some businesses continue to promote their "perfect" fitting process ...

... you can't "perfectly" fit a golf club to a swing that is always changing.

Then why should I get fitted for golf clubs?

Because a poorly fit set makes golf more difficult than it already is.

Those who believe that the value of golf clubs is over-rated, will often recite the old saying *"It's not the arrow, it's the Indian"*. To them I reply, *"I agree completely, but the Indian doesn't do so well with crooked arrows"*.

While a straight arrow does not aim or shoot itself, it does provide the Indian with the potential to hit his target a higher percentage of time. It makes hitting his target a little bit easier.

Similarly,

> *a properly fitted golf club does not aim or swing itself, but it does provide the golfer with the POTENTIAL to hit his target a higher percentage of time.*

Furthermore, an effective set composition provides the golfer with the POTENTIAL for added consistency and increased distance control – which is the essence of good golf.

So, a properly fitted set of golf clubs will NOT make me a better golfer?

Correct. You'll unfortunately still be the same golfer.

It's your "playing skills" that define your ability as a golfer, not your golf clubs. Unfortunately, even properly fitted golf clubs will not improve your playing skills.

By that I mean golf clubs do not improve your shot selection, club selection, your ability to form a positive intention, your ability to properly set up to the ball, or your ability to maintain a positive mindset throughout the shot creation process.

This is what Sam Snead meant when he said, "You cannot go into a shop and buy a good game of golf".

A properly fitted set of golf clubs makes shot creation a little easier. Nothing else.

For that reason alone, all avid golfers should play with a properly fitted set of golf clubs. Why would anyone want to make the game even more difficult than it already is?

What is the most common club fitting mistake?

Not getting properly fitted for the most important clubs in the bag.

The most important clubs in the golfer's bag are the putter, the driver, and the wedges. Yet, these clubs are most commonly either poorly fit or not fitted at all.

When customers come to my shop for a set evaluation, this is what I most often find:

A poorly fitted putter.
During a round of golf, about 40% of your shots will be putts. When the length, loft, and lie-angle of your putter complement your setup position and stroke, putting becomes easier. Yet, most golfers continue to buy expensive putters off the rack with no consideration to the specifications.

A poorly fitted set of wedges.
About one-third of your "non-putts" will be struck with one of your wedges. These are your scoring clubs. In terms of shaft length, shaft weight, lie-angle, loft, and grip size, your wedges should be a logical extension of your properly fitted iron set. Yet, golfers continue to get fitted for their iron set, but not their wedges. Which makes no sense at all.

Driver specifications that inhibit accuracy.
Hitting your average drive 10 or even 20 yards farther will NOT lower your average score, but keeping the ball in play a higher percentage of time will lower your average score. Trying to gain distance at the expense of accuracy makes no sense.

Yet, when getting fitted for a driver, golfers remain fixated on distance.

Golfers make these mistakes because they've been misled by a golf industry that is more interested in selling golf clubs than lowering handicaps.

Can I just make a few positive adjustments to the clubs I already have?

Certainly and, if needed, you should.

Making positive adjustments to your current set is not as popular as it once was. There are two reasons for this. First, it can be difficult to find a trustworthy person to work on your clubs. And second, we're now living in an era of "just buy another one".

We seldom fix anything anymore, we "just buy another one". We approach our golf clubs the same way, but we shouldn't. Here are just a few of the adjustments I make almost every day:

Adjust putter specifications.
I can often bring an old putter back to life through simply giving it a new grip and adjusting either the length, lie-angle, or loft.

Adjust driver specifications.
If the head is adjustable, I can alter the face angle, loft, and possibly lie-angle. I can also cut, extend, or replace the shaft. And, if needed, I can install a better fitting grip.

Adjust wedge specifications.
A poorly fit set of wedges can be salvaged through re-gripping and adjusting the specifications – shaft length, loft, and lie-angles.

Re-Grip sets.
Installing new, properly sized grips will give your current set an entirely new feel.

Adjust iron lie-angles.
If needed, adjusting the lie-angles of your irons can be an affordable way to make the set more playable.

Before buying a new set of golf clubs, consider making a few positive adjustments to the set you already own.

Thoughts about YOUR golf clubs

We can't solve problems by using the same kind of thinking we used when we created them.

Albert Einstein

Do I really need to be fitted for my putter?

Only if you would like to putt better.

When the shaft length, the lie-angle, and the loft of your putter each complement your setup position and stroke, you'll make square and centered contact and launch the ball on your intended line more often. Therefore, you'll putt better. Adjusting putter specifications is something I do every day. Here's what I do:

I adjust the shaft length so you can comfortably get your eyes over the ball.

After assuming a comfortable address position, you should look down and find the putter head resting directly under your eyes. From this position, it'll become easier to square the putter face to your intended line, and easier to return the putter face to square at impact. Most golfers play with a putter that is too long.

I adjust the lie angle so the putter sits flat on the ground.

The ball should be stuck in the center of the clubface, directly in-line with the club head's center of gravity – the club head's sweet spot. This is most easily accomplished when, at address, the putter head is resting flat on the ground. How a putter sits on the ground is dependent on how the golfer positions his hands. If, after adjusting the shaft length, the putter head is still not resting flat on the ground at address, I'll adjust the lie angle so that it does.

I adjust the putter's loft to better complement your stroke.

Because of its weight, a golf ball resting on the green is actually sitting down into the grass. For that reason, putters have a slight degree of loft. The goal is to strike the ball with just enough loft to launch the ball out of its resting place and get it rolling forward as quickly as possible.

How much loft your putter needs is dependent on the position of your hands at the moment of impact. If you putt with your hands well ahead of the ball, like Phil Mickelson, you'll need to add loft to your putter. And if you putt with your hands well behind the ball, like Zack Johnson, you'll need to reduce the loft on your putter. During a putter fit, I'll observe the clients address position, his stroke, and how the ball rolls on the green. Then, if needed, I'll adjust the loft of his putter.

Remember, during a round of golf,
about 40% of your shots will be putts.
Playing with a poorly fit putter makes no sense.

What driver should I be playing?

A driver that provides MAXIMUM accuracy and adequate distance.

Regardless of what you might believe, you don't have to hit your drives farther to score better. All you have to do is hit the fairway more often.

The average golfer hits his tee shot in the fairway less than half the time. His driving accuracy is poor for many reasons, one being that he uses a driver designed to maximize distance instead of accuracy.

To help a golfer hit more fairways, here are three adjustments I'll commonly make to his driver.

I'll reduce the shaft length.
When the driver shaft is too long, it becomes very difficult to make square and centered contact. As a result, the player loses both accuracy and distance. I've found that most golfers achieve the best results when using a driver with a shaft length between 43 and 44 inches. Unfortunately, most golfers carry a driver that's between 45 and 46 inches long. For that reason, I cut driver shafts down almost every day.

I'll add loft.
Golfers like low lofted drivers because they think the ball will launch lower and roll farther. And while that's true, it's also true that that most of their drives will both launch and roll farther off line. Remember, to lower your average score, you have to keep the ball in play. And while higher lofted drivers may produce less roll, they'll help you keep the ball in the fairway.

I'll adjust face angle.

Very simply stated, the "face angle" of a driver refers to the direction the club face is pointing when the driver head is soled on the ground at address. With the modern adjustable driver, I'm often able to adjust the face angle in a manner that will help to compensate for the player's most common miss. While this adjustment will seldom eliminate the slice or hook, it can make the miss significantly less severe.

While striving to maximize distance,
never sacrifice accuracy.

Should I get fitted for my wedges?

Yes, and the specifications should complement your properly fitted iron set.

Remember, about one-third of your "non-putts" will be struck with one of your wedges. They are your scoring clubs. Yet, most golfers simply buy their wedges without much thought, one at a time, off the rack. Which is why I routinely see golfers play with four wedges, each having a different brand-name, lie-angle, shaft, and grip.

The modern iron set is commonly built with a strong lofted wedge, generally 44 to 46 degrees. For this reason, I recommend that clients add at least three additional wedges to their set – a gap wedge (around 50 degrees), a sand wedge (around 55 degrees), and a lob wedge (around 60 degrees). While these wedges will vary in loft and bounce, I prefer that they have the same shaft, the same shaft length, the same lie-angle, and the same grip. In other words, I feel that wedges should be built in a set.

If your wedges are the same length, there should be a consistent 5 or 6 degree progression of lofts between each of them.

For example, if your pitching wedge is 45 degrees and you elect for a 5 degree progression, your gap wedge would be 50 degrees, your sand wedge 55 degrees, and your lob wedge 60 degrees. And if you elected for a 6 degree progression, your gap wedge would be 51 degrees, your sand wedge would be 57 degrees, and your lob wedge would be 63 degrees.

The bounce and grind of the wedges should complement the skill level and short game technique of the player. Most players need more bounce and less heel and toe relief. Their ball-striking is more consistent when they keep club face rotation to a minimum.

Golfers are always getting fitted for their irons and never their wedges, which makes little sense.

What iron design do you most often recommend?

A game improvement design with adequate loft.

When hitting an iron, average golfers seldom strike the golf ball in the middle of the club face. They also seldom make contact with the club face square to their intended target. For those two reasons, they should be playing with irons that are both forgiving and compensating.

The modern game-improvement iron head features a deep cavity back, extreme perimeter weighting, a wide sole, a thick top line, and a significant degree of hosel offset. All great features for the average golfer.

The problem is that most game improvement designs are too strong lofted.

This is because manufacturers are in the business of selling golf clubs, and distance sells. Unfortunately, when playing with a strong lofted, game-improvement set of irons, most golfers are only able to achieve a playable trajectory with the short irons.

To achieve a "playable trajectory" with a particular golf club, the player needs to be able to launch the ball high enough that it will land softly and stay on the green.

Because modern game improvement golf clubs are so strong lofted, the majority of average golfers are unable to *effectively* play the three, four or five-iron. And many are unable to *effectively* play a six or seven-iron. They just don't swing the club head fast enough.

These players really have two choices. Either play with a weaker lofted, game-improvement set of irons, or replace their mid-irons with hybrids.

What would be the best set composition for me?

The one that provides functional yardage gaps and playable trajectories throughout the bag.

When thinking about how many and what type of golf clubs you should be playing, focus on playable trajectories and functional yardage gaps.

You want at least a 10-yard gap in carry distance between each of your clubs, and you want to achieve a playable trajectory with as many clubs as possible.

Because of the head design and shaft length, you'll typically hit the ball higher and farther with a hybrid than you would with an identically lofted iron. Similarly, you'll typically hit the ball higher and farther with a fairway metal than you would with an identically lofted hybrid. With that basic understanding, you can begin to assemble a functional set of golf clubs.

When you cannot achieve a playable trajectory with an iron, replace it with a hybrid. For example, if you're unable to get your 6-iron properly elevated (launch it high enough that it will land and stay on the green), replace it with a similarly lofted hybrid.

Then, continue using hybrids until, again, you're unable to achieve a playable trajectory. At that point, replace the hybrid with a similarly lofted fairway metal. For example, if you're unable to get your 3-hybrid properly elevated, consider replacing it with a similarly lofted 7-wood.

To determine the lofts and club lengths required for you to achieve functional yardage gaps in carry distances, you'll need to work with a qualified club fitter.

While you're allowed to carry 14 golf clubs, you certainly don't have to carry that many. In fact, many of my slower swinging clients score to their full potential with only 8 clubs.

Finally, regardless of your club head speed, there is certainly nothing wrong with carrying a few specialty clubs. For example, I'm perfectly content playing with 12 clubs, but I added two specialty clubs to my set – a 64 degree wedge and a 3-iron. I seldom use these clubs, but in certain situations I'm very glad they're available.

Final Thoughts

The average golfer's problem is not so much a lack of ability as it is a lack of knowing what he should do.

Ben Hogan

Four things you need to remember about golf clubs.

While I hope you'll review this little book often, you really only need to remember these four things:

1. Golf clubs are not getting better every year.

You no longer have to worry about keeping up with the "new technology", because golf clubs are as good as they're going to get. To be deemed legal, all golf club designs have to conform to the strict guidelines established by the ruling bodies of golf - The USGA and the R&A

2.The fit is all there is. The fit is everything..

There is no best brand of golf club, so you can forget about marketing hype. Just find a trustworthy fitter that can help you identify the golf club specifications that work best for you.

3. When being fitted, remember my "Three C's".

Comfort.
The specifications of each club should complement your size, strength, and sense of feel.

Composition.
The combination of wedges, irons, hybrids, and fairway metals should provide you with playable trajectories, functional yardage gaps, and a progressive series of predictable carry distances.

Compensation.
The specifications of each club should compensate for your most common miss.

4. If you want to significantly lower your average score, you'll need to do more than improve your equipment.

Don't be misled into believing that golf clubs are more important than they really are. Golf clubs do not swing themselves. Your average golf score reflects your ball-striking ability and playing skills, not your golf clubs.

If you would like to learn more about playing skills, please read my book *Understanding Golf.*

I look forward to helping you grow your game!

Golfers are always asking me how to lower their average score. My answer is always the same – *hit fewer below average golf shots*. When you learn to do that, your average score will drop IMMEDIATELY. Regardless of your level of play.

So, how do you hit fewer below average golf shots?

Teaching students how to lower their average score through hitting fewer below average golf shots is what I do every day. My primary areas of focus are:

Eliminating golf clubs that is difficult for the student to use.
Every golf club in a student's bag should serve a specific purpose and be easy for them to use. In other words, it should be built or adjusted to both fill a need, and fit the student's size, strength, and swing motion.

Golf clubs that are easier to use provide the student with the potential to make square and centered contact, launch the ball on a playable trajectory, and carry the ball a specific distance a higher percentage of time.

Clubs that are easier to use provide the potential to hit fewer below average golf shots.

Improving the student's ball-striking skills.
Through working with each student's natural swing motion, I teach them how to expand the margin of error in every aspect of their game – putting, chipping, pitching, recovery shots, and the full swing. I do this, primarily, through teaching them impact dynamics, adjusting their setup position, and sharpening their swing focus.

As students expand their margin of error, they hit fewer below average golf shots.

Improving the student's playing skills.
On the golf course, I teach each student how to improve their playing skills – the five controllable aspects of shot creation. Those skills would be shot selection, club selection, intention, setup position, and swing focus.

As students improve their playing skills, they hit fewer below average golf shots.

Thank you so much for taking the time to read this little book. I hope it provided you with at least a few valuable insights.

I'm always available to answer any further questions you might have. I also look forward to working with you as a club maker, golf coach, or hopefully both!

Phil Moore
PhilsGolf.com
951-377-6268

Made in the USA
Monee, IL
25 July 2021